500

JOURNAL WRITING PROMPTS

Categorized Journal Prompts for Self-Discovery, Life
Reflections and Creating a Compelling Future

Disclaimer Notice:
Please note the information contained within this document is for educational and
entertainment purposes only. No warranties of any kind are expressed or implied.
Please consult a licensed professional before attempting any techniques outlined in this book.

Contents

Introduction

Anybody can feel stuck and in need of inspiration to get started or proceed with their journaling. With a large number of diversified prompts, you will be sure to find the inspiration you need within these pages.

This collection of 500 categorized journal prompts is created to help you get inspired for your self-discovering journaling. If you write a response to every prompt in this book, you will inevitably know yourself a great deal better and also most likely have had a fascinating and fulfilling journey towards your unique inner findings.

This book has prompts for all areas of life and enough for a great deal of devoted journaling-time depending on your level of activity. The prompts are categorized in a timeline starting with your memories working into the present and on to creating a compelling future. They are designed and published with the primary purpose of helping you reveal your honest and true self and challenging your beliefs.

How to use the prompts

On the next couple of pages, I will go through the different ways to journal with the prompts, and how to create a journal practice that works.

The prompts in this book are not dated, and you can pick and choose your way with the prompts as you wish.

You can choose any prompt or category of prompts you feel drawn to at any time. You might feel inspired to work with a specific section at a time; for instance, something you find to be a current theme in your life. By that, you will have easy access to prompts for every mood and matter. When you choose a specific category, you are presented with a collection of thought-provoking prompts related to this topic to get your journal practice going.

I strongly advise you not to make journaling yet another undesirable duty or task in your life that you need to complete. Have fun with it and let inspiration and curiosity be your driving force.

Also, don't ever think that what you write down needs to be perfect or even a particular anything. If you write something you don't actually mean, then no harm done. You are not going to hand it in or show it to anybody, and it's a great way to learn to be okay with making so-called mistakes.

You may feel the urge to write down pressing thoughts to begin with or to warm up a bit before starting to get into a comfortable writing zone. I suggest you write down anything whether it be sense or nonsense for the only purpose of just moving the pen or pencil on the paper. Soon you will find yourself in the right mode.

Getting started on a blank page can be a challenge. That's why prompts are so amazing. You can start by writing your immediate response to a prompt and from there see where it goes. The prompts are designed to spark your memory, make you reflect on areas of life and to help you know yourself even better. They are more than enough to fill out an entire journal and then some.

If you prefer, you can choose not to take the prompts literally but merely use them for inspiration. For instance, if one prompt says, "write down the craziest thing you ever did" and you are not sure what that is, then write about any one crazy thing you have done. See also if you can go a bit further and note down the lessons you learned from that, as well as if and how it changed your life, etc.

Notice how you feel right before and after responding to a prompt. Was the writing helpful and how so? Did you discover something new or deeper about yourself and your beliefs? Did it uplift you to write your thoughts or did it lower your energy?

I want to stress that whatever comes out of you and down onto the paper is 100% okay. If you feel uncomfortable at any point, you can always choose to let go of the writing and skip specific prompts. And if you at any time feel the need to talk to someone on your self-exploration journey, I strongly encourage you to do just that.

It can be a fun experience to later read through your journal to notice your development and any possible change in yourself, your memories and your beliefs. For this reason, remember to date the pages.

I have lined this book for you to use at as your journal. However, I'm sure that in some cases you will need more space than provided and you can continue in another journal. When you purchase this book, you have the option to download the kindle version for free as a little gift from me to you. In that way, you can have the prompts handy on your phone or kindle reader at all times and continue journaling.

Without further ado, let's get journaling . . .

MEMORIES

1. What retro devices to you remember appreciating and would love to have in your life today?

Date: _____

2. Write about something you thought was impossible, but then it happened anyway.

Date: _____

3. What do you miss the most and why? It can be anybody or anything, external or internal.

Date: _____

_____
_____
_____
_____
_____
_____
_____
_____
_____
_____
_____

4. With what are you happy to be done doing?

Date: _____

_____
_____
_____
_____
_____
_____
_____
_____
_____
_____
_____

5. If you could change a decision you made in your past, what would it be and how would it change your life?

Date: _____

_____
_____
_____
_____
_____
_____
_____
_____
_____
_____

6. Write about the best week you had during your school years.

Date: _____

_____
_____
_____
_____
_____
_____
_____
_____
_____
_____
_____

7. Write about the first time you ever won anything.

Date: _____

8. Write about the most remarkable thing you have ever won.

Date: _____

9. What was your favorite topic in school? What made it exciting?

Date: _____

_____
_____
_____
_____
_____
_____
_____
_____
_____
_____
_____

10. Write about the five happiest times in your childhood.

Date: _____

_____
_____
_____
_____
_____
_____
_____
_____
_____
_____
_____

11. Rewrite your childhood to make the way you would want it to be.

Date: _____

_____
_____
_____
_____
_____
_____
_____
_____
_____
_____
_____
_____

12. Write the things you wished most for when you were a child.

Date: _____

_____
_____
_____
_____
_____
_____
_____
_____
_____
_____
_____

13. Write about the best party you ever attended.

Date: _____

_____
_____
_____
_____
_____
_____
_____
_____
_____
_____
_____
_____
_____

14. Write about the last time you did something entirely new.

Date: _____

_____
_____
_____
_____
_____
_____
_____
_____
_____
_____
_____
_____

15. Write about a time you felt alone.

Date: _____

_____
_____
_____
_____
_____
_____
_____
_____
_____
_____
_____
_____

16. Write about a time you didn't feel alone.

Date: _____

_____
_____
_____
_____
_____
_____
_____
_____
_____
_____

17. Write down all the compliments you can remember receiving.

Date: _____

_____
_____
_____
_____
_____
_____
_____
_____
_____
_____

18. Write about something you have experienced that you couldn't explain logically.

Date: _____

_____
_____
_____
_____
_____
_____
_____
_____
_____

19. Write about a time you broke a rule or law that made you feel
    genuinely guilty.

Date: _____

_____

_____

_____

_____

_____

_____

_____

_____

_____

_____

_____

_____

20.   What was the hardest thing you ever had to accept?

Date: _____

_____

_____

_____

_____

_____

_____

_____

_____

_____

_____

_____

21. Write about the best time you ever had on the beach.

Date: _____

_____
_____
_____
_____
_____
_____
_____
_____
_____
_____
_____

22. What's the most valuable thing you have ever found and what did you do with it?

Date: _____

_____
_____
_____
_____
_____
_____
_____
_____
_____
_____
_____

23. Write about the last time you couldn't stop laughing.

Date: _____

_____
_____
_____
_____
_____
_____
_____
_____
_____
_____
_____

24. Write about your childhood love life.

Date: _____

_____
_____
_____
_____
_____
_____
_____
_____
_____
_____

25. What was the hardest thing you ever had to learn?

Date: _____

_____
_____
_____
_____
_____
_____
_____
_____
_____
_____
_____

26. What was the most challenging thing you ever had to do?

Date: _____

_____
_____
_____
_____
_____
_____
_____
_____
_____
_____
_____

27. What was the toughest thing you ever had to say?

Date: _____

_____
_____
_____
_____
_____
_____
_____
_____
_____
_____
_____
_____

28. Write about a time you reluctantly had to give up something, but in hindsight, it was the right thing to give it up.

Date: _____

_____
_____
_____
_____
_____
_____
_____
_____
_____
_____

29. Write about a time when a seemingly bad event happened, but it turned out for the best in the end.

Date: _____

_____
_____
_____
_____
_____
_____
_____
_____
_____
_____
_____

30. Write about a time you got what you wanted only to find that you didn't want that after all.

Date: _____

_____
_____
_____
_____
_____
_____
_____
_____
_____
_____

31. What did you do and think more of 10 years ago?

Date: _____

_____
_____
_____
_____
_____
_____
_____
_____
_____
_____
_____
_____

32. What did you do and think less of 10 years ago?

Date: _____

_____
_____
_____
_____
_____
_____
_____
_____
_____
_____
_____
_____

Write your experience with the longest time you ever went without:

33. Food?

Date: _____

_____
_____
_____
_____
_____
_____
_____
_____
_____
_____
_____
_____

34. Water?

Date: _____

_____
_____
_____
_____
_____
_____
_____
_____
_____
_____
_____
_____
_____

35. Sleep?

Date: _____

_____
_____
_____
_____
_____
_____
_____
_____
_____
_____
_____

36. Company?

Date: _____

_____
_____
_____
_____
_____
_____
_____
_____
_____
_____
_____
_____

37. Wearing clothes?

Date: _____

38. Heat?

Date: _____

39. Nature?

Date: _____

_____
_____
_____
_____
_____
_____
_____
_____
_____
_____
_____

40. A computer?

Date: _____

_____
_____
_____
_____
_____
_____
_____
_____
_____
_____
_____

41. Your phone?

Date: _____

_____
_____
_____
_____
_____
_____
_____
_____
_____
_____
_____

42. Your bed?

Date: _____

_____
_____
_____
_____
_____
_____
_____
_____
_____
_____
_____
_____

43. A partner?

Date: _____

_____
_____
_____
_____
_____
_____
_____
_____
_____
_____

Finish the sentence:

44. The stupidest thing I ever did...

Date: _____

_____
_____
_____
_____
_____
_____
_____
_____
_____
_____
_____

45.   The most terrifying moment of my life was . . .

Date: _____

_____
_____
_____
_____
_____
_____
_____
_____
_____
_____
_____
_____
_____

46.   The most fun I've ever had . . .

Date: _____

_____
_____
_____
_____
_____
_____
_____
_____
_____
_____
_____
_____

47.   The most surprised I've ever been . . .

Date: _____

_____
_____
_____
_____
_____
_____
_____
_____
_____
_____
_____

48. The most disappointed I've ever been . . .

Date: _____

_____
_____
_____
_____
_____
_____
_____
_____
_____
_____

49. The best party I ever went to was . . .

Date: _____

50. The best night out I ever had was . . .

Date: _____

51. The thing I miss most about _____ is . . .

Date: _____

52. The thing I miss least about _____ is . . .

Date: _____

DAILY REFLECTIONS

53.   What's the kindest thing you did today?

Date: _____

54.   What's the kindest thing you witnessed today?

Date: _____

55.   What do you wish hadn't happened today and why?

Date: _____

_____

_____

_____

_____

_____

_____

_____

_____

_____

_____

_____

56.   What did you enjoy today that you will do again tomorrow?

Date: _____

_____

_____

_____

_____

_____

_____

_____

_____

_____

_____

57.   How did you express love today?

Date: _____

58.   What about this day makes you feel grateful?

Date: _____

59.   Make a list of how much time you spend on different things today. Make sure the time adds up to 24 hours.

Date: _____

_____
_____
_____
_____
_____
_____
_____
_____
_____
_____
_____
_____

60.   Make a list of everything you ate and drank today.

Date: _____

_____
_____
_____
_____
_____
_____
_____
_____
_____
_____
_____

61.   If this day had a theme what would it be?

Date: _____

_____
_____
_____
_____
_____
_____
_____
_____
_____
_____
_____
_____

62.   On a scale from 1-10 how was your day and why was it that way?

Date: _____

_____
_____
_____
_____
_____
_____
_____
_____
_____
_____
_____
_____

63.   What was your favorite thing about today?

Date: _____

_____
_____
_____
_____
_____
_____
_____
_____
_____
_____
_____
_____

64.   What was your least favorite thing about today?

Date: _____

_____
_____
_____
_____
_____
_____
_____
_____
_____
_____
_____
_____

65.   What did you wish you had said to another person today had you been fast enough?

Date: _____

_____

_____

_____

_____

_____

_____

_____

_____

_____

_____

_____

66.   What were the funniest things you said or heard someone say today?

Date: _____

_____

_____

_____

_____

_____

_____

_____

_____

_____

_____

_____

67.   What was the overall theme of today and how did it play out?

Date: _____

68.   In what situation(s) were you not completely honest today?

Date: _____

69.   What would you like to change about today?

Date: _____

_____
_____
_____
_____
_____
_____
_____
_____
_____
_____
_____

70.   What songs were stuck in your head today? How do you feel about those songs?

Date: _____

_____
_____
_____
_____
_____
_____
_____
_____
_____
_____
_____

71.   What did you learn today?

Date: _____

72.   What were you most surprised about today?

Date: _____

WEEKLY REFLECTIONS

73. What A-HA moments did you have this week?

Date: _____

_____
_____
_____
_____
_____
_____
_____
_____
_____
_____
_____

74. Who contributed to making your week better?

Date: _____

_____
_____
_____
_____
_____
_____
_____
_____
_____
_____
_____

75. What do you wish hadn't happened this week?

Date: _____

_____
_____
_____
_____
_____
_____
_____
_____
_____
_____
_____

76. What did you do this week that got you closer to reaching your goals?

Date: _____

_____
_____
_____
_____
_____
_____
_____
_____
_____
_____

77. Is there anything you did this week that you will do differently in the future?

Date: _____

_____
_____
_____
_____
_____
_____
_____
_____
_____
_____
_____

78. What did you do this week that got you closer to reaching your goals?

Date: _____

_____
_____
_____
_____
_____
_____
_____
_____
_____
_____
_____

79. What was your biggest joy this week and why?

Date: _____

_____
_____
_____
_____
_____
_____
_____
_____
_____
_____
_____
_____

80. How did you procrastinate this week?

Date: _____

_____
_____
_____
_____
_____
_____
_____
_____
_____
_____
_____
_____

81. How were you good to yourself this week?

Date: _____

_____
_____
_____
_____
_____
_____
_____
_____
_____
_____
_____
_____

82. How did you overcome procrastination this week?

Date: _____

_____
_____
_____
_____
_____
_____
_____
_____
_____
_____
_____
_____

83. What did you get better at this week?

Date: _____

_____

_____

_____

_____

_____

_____

_____

_____

_____

_____

84. What was your funniest moment this week?

Date: _____

_____

_____

_____

_____

_____

_____

_____

_____

_____

_____

85. How did you make an impact on another person's life this week?

Date: _____

----

86. What websites did you visit most frequently this week?

Date: _____

----

87. Write about your best conversation this week.

Date: _____

_____
_____
_____
_____
_____
_____
_____
_____
_____
_____

88. Write about something you were given this week.

Date: _____

_____
_____
_____
_____
_____
_____
_____
_____
_____
_____

89. What rules or laws did you break this week?

Date: _____

_____
_____
_____
_____
_____
_____
_____
_____
_____
_____
_____

90. What were you most surprised about this week?

Date: _____

_____
_____
_____
_____
_____
_____
_____
_____
_____
_____
_____

91. Did something seemingly regretful turn out great?

Date: _____

_____
_____
_____
_____
_____
_____
_____
_____
_____
_____
_____
_____

92. What did you expect to turn out differently?

Date: _____

_____
_____
_____
_____
_____
_____
_____
_____
_____
_____
_____
_____

CONFESSIONS

93. What do you feel guilty about and for which you wish you could be forgiven?

Date: _____

_____
_____
_____
_____
_____
_____
_____
_____
_____
_____
_____

94. What's the worst thing you've ever done?

Date: _____

_____
_____
_____
_____
_____
_____
_____
_____
_____
_____

95. About what do you want no one to know?

Date: _____

_____
_____
_____
_____
_____
_____
_____
_____
_____
_____
_____
_____

96. What's the most shameful thing you've ever done?

Date: _____

_____
_____
_____
_____
_____
_____
_____
_____
_____
_____
_____
_____

97. What's the craziest thing you have ever done?

Date: _____

_____
_____
_____
_____
_____
_____
_____
_____
_____
_____
_____
_____

98. How do you feel about death and mortality?

Date: _____

_____
_____
_____
_____
_____
_____
_____
_____
_____
_____
_____

99. Have you ever felt that you needed to change something about yourself? What and why?

Date: _____

_____
_____
_____
_____
_____
_____
_____
_____
_____
_____
_____

100.   What is something no one would really believe about you?

Date: _____

_____
_____
_____
_____
_____
_____
_____
_____
_____
_____

101. What do you not like about kids?

Date: _____

102.   How have you taken advantage of somebody else?

Date: _____

MINDFULNESS

103.   What is on your mind right now?

Date: _____

104.   Look around and describe your surroundings.

Date: _____

105.   Listen to the sounds around you and write them down as you hear them.

Date: _____

_____

_____

_____

_____

_____

_____

_____

_____

_____

_____

_____

106.   Find something near you that you think is beautiful and describe it in detail.

Date: _____

_____

_____

_____

_____

_____

_____

_____

_____

_____

_____

107.   What does it feel like in your body right now? Write down all your sensations.

Date: _____

_____

_____

_____

_____

_____

_____

_____

_____

_____

_____

_____

108.   What makes you less present in the now?

Date: _____

_____

_____

_____

_____

_____

_____

_____

_____

_____

_____

109.   Who do you find to be most present in the now? What does he or she do differently than others?

Date: _____

_____
_____
_____
_____
_____
_____
_____
_____
_____
_____
_____

110.   In what situations do you find yourself to be most present in the here and now?

Date: _____

_____
_____
_____
_____
_____
_____
_____
_____
_____
_____
_____

111.   What can you do the coming days to be more present in the now?

Date: _____

_____
_____
_____
_____
_____
_____
_____
_____
_____
_____
_____
_____

112.   How would you explain being present to a child?

Date: _____

_____
_____
_____
_____
_____
_____
_____
_____
_____
_____
_____

Finish the sentence:

113.   I lose all sense of time when I . . .

Date: _____

114.   When I am on my own, I love to . . .

Date: _____

YOUR FAVORITES

115.   List your favorite movies.

Date: _____

_____
_____
_____
_____
_____
_____
_____
_____
_____
_____
_____

116.   List your favorite songs.

Date: _____

_____
_____
_____
_____
_____
_____
_____
_____
_____
_____
_____

117.   Categorize your favorite songs into what you like to hear while you are in different moods.

Date: _____

118. What are your favorite rituals or routines in your life right now?

Date: _____

119. List ten things you can't go without in a day.

Date: _____

120. List your favorite things to wear.

Date: _____

121.   What is your favorite TV show at the moment and why?

Date: _____

122.   If you went to a third world country what are three things you would absolutely take with you?

Date: _____

123.   What has been your favorite holiday and what made it
       special?

Date: _____

_____
_____
_____
_____
_____
_____
_____
_____
_____
_____
_____
_____

124.   List is your favorite sayings at the moment.

Date: _____

_____
_____
_____
_____
_____
_____
_____
_____
_____
_____
_____

125.   What are your favorite things in general?

Date: _____

126.   List your five favorite sources of inspiration at the moment.

Date: _____

127.   Write down your favorite pranks.

Date: _____

128.   What are your favorite topics to talk about with your friends or family?

Date: _____

129.   What are your favorite websites and why?

Date: _____

130.   What are your favorite blogs and what value do they give you?

Date: _____

131.   What are your favorite YouTube channels and what value do they give you?

Date: _____

_____
_____
_____
_____
_____
_____
_____
_____
_____
_____
_____

132.   What has always been your all-time favorite hobby and why do you love it?

Date: _____

_____
_____
_____
_____
_____
_____
_____
_____
_____
_____
_____

133.   What is your favorite fairytale and what do you like about it?

Date: _____

_____
_____
_____
_____
_____
_____
_____
_____
_____
_____

134.   Think about your favorite sounds. When and how you listen to them?

Date: _____

_____
_____
_____
_____
_____
_____
_____
_____
_____
_____

135.   Write about your favorite indoor activities.

Date: _____

_____
_____
_____
_____
_____
_____
_____
_____
_____
_____
_____
_____

136.   Write about your favorite outdoor activities.

Date: _____

_____
_____
_____
_____
_____
_____
_____
_____
_____
_____
_____

MORALS AND ETHICS

137.   How do you feel about plastic surgery?

Date: _____

138.   What is your take on euthanasia?

Date: _____

139.   When is it okay to not fulfill one's obligations if ever?

Date: _____

_____
_____
_____
_____
_____
_____
_____
_____
_____
_____

140.   What is your take on charity?

Date: _____

_____
_____
_____
_____
_____
_____
_____
_____
_____
_____

141.   When do you feel an obligation to help people in need?

Date: _____

_____
_____
_____
_____
_____
_____
_____
_____
_____
_____
_____
_____

142.   Do you think TV shows can be damaging? If yes, how so? If no, why not?

Date: _____

_____
_____
_____
_____
_____
_____
_____
_____
_____
_____
_____

143.   When is it not okay to be selfish?

Date: _____

144.   What is your take on nuclear power?

Date: _____

145.   What responsibilities do you think the media have if any?

Date: _____

_____
_____
_____
_____
_____
_____
_____
_____
_____
_____
_____

146.   What do you think about the death penalty?

Date: _____

_____
_____
_____
_____
_____
_____
_____
_____
_____
_____
_____

147.   How do you feel about weapons?

Date: _____

148.   What is your take on the gun laws in your country?

Date: _____

149.   What do you think about hunting?

Date: _____

_____
_____
_____
_____
_____
_____
_____
_____
_____
_____
_____

150.   What is your take on abortion?

Date: _____

_____
_____
_____
_____
_____
_____
_____
_____
_____
_____
_____

151.   What is your take on organ donation?

Date: _____

_____
_____
_____
_____
_____
_____
_____
_____
_____
_____
_____

152.   What are the obligations of each individual regarding the
climate?

Date: _____

_____
_____
_____
_____
_____
_____
_____
_____
_____
_____
_____

153.   Is there a right way to fire an employee, and what difference does it make if any?

Date: _____

154.   Do rich people have obligations that poor people do not have?

Date: _____

155.   How should elderly people be treated?

Date: _____

_____

_____

_____

_____

_____

_____

_____

_____

_____

_____

156.   Do you think there should be a limit to the use of cell phones and computers and how so?

Date: _____

_____

_____

_____

_____

_____

_____

_____

_____

_____

_____

157.   What is your take on general consumption? Should there be a limit?

Date: _____

_____

_____

_____

_____

_____

_____

_____

_____

_____

_____

_____

158.   List things you would never do.

Date: _____

_____

_____

_____

_____

_____

_____

_____

_____

_____

_____

_____

HAPPINESS

159.   What immediately comes to mind when you read the word "happiness?"

Date: _____

160.   Write the best things about being your age.

Date: _____

161.   List all the positive things you can think of about a person
you sincerely dislike.

Date: _____

162.   What matters most to you in your life?

Date: _____

163.   List all the things you can think of that instantly makes
        you smile

Date: _____

_____

_____

_____

_____

_____

_____

_____

_____

_____

_____

_____

164.   Write down things you like to do just for fun.

Date: _____

_____

_____

_____

_____

_____

_____

_____

_____

_____

_____

_____

165.   Write down the best news you heard lately.

Date: _____

166.   Finish this sentence: I am so happy that I have...

Date: _____

167.   Finish this sentence: I am so happy that I don't have...

Date: _____

_____
_____
_____
_____
_____
_____
_____
_____
_____
_____

168.   Whose level of happiness inspires you and why?

Date: _____

_____
_____
_____
_____
_____
_____
_____
_____
_____
_____

169.   Write about a time you were laughing so hard you couldn't stop.

Date: _____

_____

_____

_____

_____

_____

_____

_____

_____

_____

_____

170.   How would you explain happiness to a child?

Date: _____

_____

_____

_____

_____

_____

_____

_____

_____

_____

_____

171.   Write down what is better in your life now than a year ago.

Date: _____

172.   Write down what makes you happy to look at.

Date: _____

173.   Write down what you are really happy is no longer is a part
in your life.

Date: _____

_____

_____

_____

_____

_____

_____

_____

_____

_____

_____

174.   Write down the outline to the happiest day you can
imagine.

Date: _____

_____

_____

_____

_____

_____

_____

_____

_____

_____

175.   Write down something that made you smile today.

Date: _____

176.   Write down all the things you associate with happiness
that doesn't cost a thing.

Date: _____

GRATITUDE AND APPRECIATION

177.   What places are you really grateful exist?

Date: _____

_____
_____
_____
_____
_____
_____
_____
_____
_____
_____
_____

178.   What buildings are you really grateful exist?

Date: _____

_____
_____
_____
_____
_____
_____
_____
_____
_____
_____
_____

179.   What shops are you really grateful for?

Date: _____

180.   What products are you really grateful for?

Date: _____

181.   List the three things you are most grateful for right at this
        moment.

Date: _____

182.   Express your gratitude toward yourself

Date: _____

183.   List 5 small things that you are grateful for

Date: _____

184.   What are the best things about living in your country?

Date: _____

185. What are the best things about your family?

Date: _____

_____
_____
_____
_____
_____
_____
_____
_____
_____
_____
_____

186. What are the best things about the home you live in?

Date: _____

_____
_____
_____
_____
_____
_____
_____
_____
_____
_____
_____

187.   Which 3 possessions really helps you to make your life easier and how so?

Date: _____

_____
_____
_____
_____
_____
_____
_____
_____
_____
_____

188.   Write about an invention from the last decade that you are very grateful for.

Date: _____

_____
_____
_____
_____
_____
_____
_____
_____
_____

189.   Write your thoughts about gratitude and what it means to you.

Date: _____

_____

_____

_____

_____

_____

_____

_____

_____

_____

_____

190.   Imagine that all others had it worse than you. What would you appreciate more about your life then?

Date: _____

_____

_____

_____

_____

_____

_____

_____

_____

_____

_____

191.   List all the people closest to you. Write what you appreciate about each one of them individually.

Date: _____

_____

_____

_____

_____

_____

_____

_____

_____

_____

_____

_____

192.   List the books you appreciate the most.

Date: _____

_____

_____

_____

_____

_____

_____

_____

_____

_____

_____

_____

193.   List the songs you appreciate the most.

Date: _____

_____
_____
_____
_____
_____
_____
_____
_____
_____
_____
_____

194.   What do you appreciate about nature?

Date: _____

_____
_____
_____
_____
_____
_____
_____
_____
_____
_____
_____

195.   What do you appreciate about big cities?

Date: _____

_____
_____
_____
_____
_____
_____
_____
_____
_____
_____
_____
_____

196.   What do you appreciate about the country side?

Date: _____

_____
_____
_____
_____
_____
_____
_____
_____
_____
_____
_____

197.   What do you appreciate about the work you are currently engaged in?

Date: _____

198.   Make a list of 10 things that instantly puts a smile on your face.

Date: _____

RITUALS

199.   Write down all the rituals you have during a day that you can think of.

Date: _____

200.   Write down your morning ritual.

Date: _____

201.   Write about your favorite ritual.

Date: _____

202.   Write down you bad habits and why you think you have them.

Date: _____

203.   Write some of other people's rituals that you don't have yourself.

Date: _____

204.   Which TV-shows do you watch habitually?

Date: _____

WRITE A LETTER

205.   Write a letter to the person you currently disagree with the most.

Date: _____

206.   Write a letter to a friend mentioning the things you never say because it would be rude or inappropriate.

Date: _____

207.   Write a letter to both your parents for them to read together.

Date: _____

_____
_____
_____
_____
_____
_____
_____
_____
_____
_____
_____

208.   Write a letter to a famous person you would like to be friends with.

Date: _____

_____
_____
_____
_____
_____
_____
_____
_____
_____
_____
_____

209.   Write a letter to your boss.

Date: _____

_____
_____
_____
_____
_____
_____
_____
_____
_____
_____
_____
_____

210.   Write a letter to a friend you lost but wish was still in your life.

Date: _____

_____
_____
_____
_____
_____
_____
_____
_____
_____
_____
_____
_____

211.   Write a letter to your favorite teacher in school about your life now.

Date: _____

_____
_____
_____
_____
_____
_____
_____
_____
_____
_____
_____

212.   Write a letter to your first boyfriend or girlfriend.

Date: _____

_____
_____
_____
_____
_____
_____
_____
_____
_____
_____

213. Write a letter to yourself about how much you respect and value who you are.

Date: _____

_____
_____
_____
_____
_____
_____
_____
_____
_____
_____
_____
_____

Finish the letter:

214. Dear past me...

Date: _____

_____
_____
_____
_____
_____
_____
_____
_____
_____
_____
_____

215.   Dear future me...

Date: _____

_____
_____
_____
_____
_____
_____
_____
_____
_____
_____
_____
_____

216.   Dear mom...

Date: _____

_____
_____
_____
_____
_____
_____
_____
_____
_____
_____
_____

217.   Dear dad...

Date: _____

218.   Dear God...

Date: _____

SPIRITUALITY

219.   What does it mean to you to be spiritual?

Date: _____

220.   How are you spiritual?

Date: _____

221.   Write down your understanding of the difference between religion and spirituality.

Date: _____

_____

_____

_____

_____

_____

_____

_____

_____

_____

_____

_____

222.   What are your thoughts on reincarnation?

Date: _____

_____

_____

_____

_____

_____

_____

_____

_____

_____

_____

223.   What do you feel certain about but can't explain rationally?

Date: _____

_____

_____

_____

_____

_____

_____

_____

_____

_____

_____

224.   What spiritual aspects do you not believe in and what are your thoughts on that?

Date: _____

225.   What could be a good spiritual practice for you?

Date: _____

226.   Write down everything you relate to God.

Date: _____

227.   Do you believe things happen for a reason and why/why not?

Date: _____

228.   Write down your values and what you believe to be right.

Date: _____

229.   What is the most spiritual experience you have had?

Date: _____

230.   Which spiritual experiences would you like to have more of?

Date: _____

231.   Research the term "spirituality" and write down the definition of it in your own words.

Date: _____

_____
_____
_____
_____
_____
_____
_____
_____
_____
_____
_____

232.   Wisdom is...

Date: _____

_____
_____
_____
_____
_____
_____
_____
_____
_____
_____
_____
_____

233.   Where does wisdom come from?

Date: _____

234.   What are your thoughts about the "law of attraction"?

Date: _____

235.   Which places and people make you feel like you belong there?

Date: _____

236.   Do you think we have a purpose from birth or that we are supposed to create it entirely ourselves?

Date: _____

PERSONAL DEVELOPMENT

237.   What does it mean to you to be a strong person?

Date: _____

238.   How do you "recharge your batteries"? Alone or with people? What do you prefer doing while recharging?

Date: _____

239.   Write down 5 sentences you need to live by.

Date: _____

240.   Write down 10 defining life lessons you have learned over the past 10 years.

Date: _____

241.   List five things you'd do if you weren't so afraid.

Date: _____

242.   What does forgiveness mean to you?

Date: _____

243.   Who do you need to forgive and for what?

Date: _____

244.   What is your take on making mistakes?

Date: _____

245.   How do you move on from making a mistake?

Date: _____

246.   Write about the next thing you would like to learn.

Date: _____

247.   What do you need most in your life that should be there?

Date: _____

_____

_____

_____

_____

_____

_____

_____

_____

_____

_____

248.   What are you jealous about, honestly?

Date: _____

_____

_____

_____

_____

_____

_____

_____

_____

_____

_____

_____

249.   How would your best friend describe you?

Date: _____

_____

_____

_____

_____

_____

_____

_____

_____

_____

_____

_____

_____

250.   How would an average stranger that met you at a dinner party describe you?

Date: _____

_____

_____

_____

_____

_____

_____

_____

_____

_____

_____

_____

251.   What do you need to say no to at the moment?

Date: _____

---

252.   What would you never do again if you didn't have to and why?

Date: _____

---

253.   Who would you like to trade lives with for a day and why?

Date: _____

_____
_____
_____
_____
_____
_____
_____
_____
_____
_____
_____

254.   Write something you would like to do but couldn't possibly because of the type of person you are.

Date: _____

_____
_____
_____
_____
_____
_____
_____
_____
_____
_____
_____

255.   How would you dress if you were truly authentic?

Date: _____

256.   What does "taking responsibility" really mean?

Date: _____

257.   What do you not want to take responsibility for but should?

Date: _____

258.   Your 10 most important values.

Date: _____

259.   Your 5 most important values.

Date: _____

260.   How old do you feel and why?

Date: _____

261.   What do you not fully accept about yourself?

Date: _____

_____
_____
_____
_____
_____
_____
_____
_____
_____
_____
_____

262.   How and what would you like to play now as an adult?

Date: _____

_____
_____
_____
_____
_____
_____
_____
_____
_____
_____
_____

263.   If you could go back 10 years and relive those years. What would you do differently and what would you do the same?

Date: _____

_____
_____
_____
_____
_____
_____
_____
_____
_____
_____
_____

264.   How can you strengthen yourself?

Date: _____

_____
_____
_____
_____
_____
_____
_____
_____
_____
_____
_____
_____

265.   What can you eliminate from your life or at least minimize to be better able to focus on the things you want and that are important?

Date: _____

_____
_____
_____
_____
_____
_____
_____
_____
_____
_____
_____
_____

266.   What would you like to give up being good at?

Date: _____

_____
_____
_____
_____
_____
_____
_____
_____
_____
_____
_____

267.   What things do you find impossible but wish they weren't?

Date: _____

_____
_____
_____
_____
_____
_____
_____
_____
_____
_____
_____

268.   What can you see other people suffer under that you don't?

Date: _____

_____
_____
_____
_____
_____
_____
_____
_____
_____
_____
_____

269.   What part of you do you think is very rare?

Date: _____

270.   What do you care about now that you didn't one year ago?

Date: _____

271.   What do you use to care about that you don't anymore?

Date: _____

272.   Which efforts seems worth it?

Date: _____

273.   Which efforts don't seem worth it?

Date: _____

274.   What does "having a balanced life" mean to you?

Date: _____

275. How has getting older helped you deal with challenges in life?

Date: _____

---

276. If you could go back to any age in your life and live again what age would you go back to and why?

Date: _____

277.   How could you become more resourceful?

Date: _____

278.   What things are you procrastinating on at the moment?

Date: _____

279.   What are your typical excuses when you don't get things done?

Date: _____

_____
_____
_____
_____
_____
_____
_____
_____
_____
_____
_____

280.   How can you be more productive?

Date: _____

_____
_____
_____
_____
_____
_____
_____
_____
_____
_____
_____

281.   Who is the most productive person you know or know of?
How are they productive?

Date: _____

_____
_____
_____
_____
_____
_____
_____
_____
_____
_____
_____

282.   What would you do if there was no audience?

Date: _____

_____
_____
_____
_____
_____
_____
_____
_____
_____
_____

283.   Write about the last time you did something brave

Date: _____

284.   What do you think is necessary in life?

Date: _____

Finish the sentence:

285.   The thing that is currently hardest for me is...

Date: _____

286.   I know a lot about...

Date: _____

287.   Other people seem to think I am good at...

Date: _____

_____

_____

_____

_____

_____

_____

_____

_____

_____

_____

288.   In reality, I am good at...

Date: _____

_____

_____

_____

_____

_____

_____

_____

_____

_____

_____

_____

289.   Generally, I really like to...

Date: _____

_____
_____
_____
_____
_____
_____
_____
_____
_____
_____
_____

290.   I hate_____because

Date: _____

_____
_____
_____
_____
_____
_____
_____
_____
_____
_____
_____

291.   I will never_____because

Date: _____

_____
_____
_____
_____
_____
_____
_____
_____
_____
_____
_____

292.   Within the next month I will...

Date: _____

_____
_____
_____
_____
_____
_____
_____
_____
_____
_____
_____

293.   Within the next week I will...

Date: _____

_____
_____
_____
_____
_____
_____
_____
_____
_____
_____
_____

294.   When I have a look around in my home, it is very obvious
that I...

Date: _____

_____
_____
_____
_____
_____
_____
_____
_____
_____
_____
_____

295.   Right now, I'm not willing to...

Date: _____

296.   If I didn't worry about the future at all, I would...

Date: _____

297.   If I had enough time I would...

Date: _____

298.   I simply love to...

Date: _____

299.   I love to talk about...

Date: _____

_____
_____
_____
_____
_____
_____
_____
_____
_____
_____
_____

300.   I'm willing to go all the way to...

Date: _____

_____
_____
_____
_____
_____
_____
_____
_____
_____
_____

301.   Keeping a journal is good for...

Date: _____

302.   5 years ago, I never thought

Date: _____

303.   The things about myself I am most satisfied with are...

Date: _____

_____
_____
_____
_____
_____
_____
_____
_____
_____
_____

304.   The role I would most like to play in a movie would be...

Date: _____

_____
_____
_____
_____
_____
_____
_____
_____
_____

305.   The thing I look most forward to right now...

Date: _____

_____
_____
_____
_____
_____
_____
_____
_____
_____
_____
_____

306.   The things I am most fascinated about at the moment...

Date: _____

_____
_____
_____
_____
_____
_____
_____
_____
_____
_____
_____

DEALING WITH EMOTIONS

307.   What are the three most dominant emotions in your life right now?

Date: _____

308.   Write about the last time you said or thought "WOW".

Date: _____

309.   How can you best support yourself when you feel negative emotions?

Date: _____

_____
_____
_____
_____
_____
_____
_____
_____
_____
_____
_____

310.   What is sure to make you cry?

Date: _____

_____
_____
_____
_____
_____
_____
_____
_____
_____
_____
_____

311.   How does the weather effect your mood?

Date: _____

_____
_____
_____
_____
_____
_____
_____
_____
_____
_____

312.   How do you feel about revenge in general?

Date: _____

_____
_____
_____
_____
_____
_____
_____
_____
_____
_____

313.   Write down your irrational fears

Date: _____

314.   What emotions would you like to feel more of?

Date: _____

315.   What emotions would you like to feel less?

Date: _____

316.   Who are you jealous of and why?

Date: _____

317. Write about a time when your emotions took over.

Date: _____

_____
_____
_____
_____
_____
_____
_____
_____
_____
_____

318. Write down the things that make you feel energized.

Date: _____

_____
_____
_____
_____
_____
_____
_____
_____
_____
_____

319.   Write down the things that make you feel relaxed.

Date: _____

_____
_____
_____
_____
_____
_____
_____
_____
_____
_____
_____

320.   Write down the things that make you feel rejuvenated.

Date: _____

_____
_____
_____
_____
_____
_____
_____
_____
_____
_____

321.   Write down the things that make you feel loved

Date: _____

322.   Write down the things that makes you feel excited

Date: _____

323. What gives you anxiety? When do you get overwhelmed with anxious thinking?

Date: _____

324. When you feel good about yourself, how do you speak and what do you say?

Date: _____

325.   When you feel good about yourself, what don't you say?

Date: _____

_____
_____
_____
_____
_____
_____
_____
_____
_____
_____

326.   When you feel good about yourself, how does your home
look like?

Date: _____

_____
_____
_____
_____
_____
_____
_____
_____
_____
_____

327.   When you feel good about yourself, what do you eat?

Date: _____

328.   When you feel good about yourself, what do you always do?

Date: _____

329.   When you feel good about yourself, what do you never do?

Date: _____

330.   What are your insecurities?

Date: _____

331.   When you feel good about yourself, who do you spent time with?

Date: _____

_____

_____

_____

_____

_____

_____

_____

_____

_____

_____

332.   In what situations and with whom do you feel like you have to compromise yourself

Date: _____

_____

_____

_____

_____

_____

_____

_____

_____

_____

_____

333.   How do you usually react when you feel fear?

Date: _____

334.   What do you think is the cure for fear?

Date: _____

335.   In what way do you feel wrong?

Date: _____

336.   In what way do you feel right?

Date: _____

Finish the sentence:

337.   I feel most comfortable in my own skin when...

Date: _____

338.   My biggest concerns about the future...

Date: _____

QUOTES

Write your thoughts on these quotes:

339.   "I make myself rich by making my wants few" – Henry
Davis Thoreau

Date: _____

_____

_____

_____

_____

_____

_____

_____

_____

_____

_____

_____

340.   "To live is the rarest thing in the world. Most people just
exist" – Oscar Wilde

Date: _____

_____

_____

_____

_____

_____

_____

_____

_____

_____

_____

341.   "All great changes are preceded by chaos" – Deepak Chopra

Date: _____

342.   "You are responsible for your own happiness" – Unknown

Date: _____

343.   "It's better to be feared than loved if you cannot be both" - Niccolò Machiavelli

Date: _____

344.   "It's far better to be alone than to be in bad company" – George Washington

Date: _____

345.   "Happiness can exist only in acceptance" – George Orwell

Date: _____

345.   "The only true wisdom is in knowing you know nothing" – Socrates

Date: _____

347.   "Life isn't about finding yourself. Life is about creating yourself" - George Bernard Shaw

Date: _____

_____

_____

_____

_____

_____

_____

_____

_____

_____

_____

348.   "Life's most persistent and urgent question is, 'What are you doing for others?'" - Martin Luther King

Date: _____

_____

_____

_____

_____

_____

_____

_____

_____

_____

_____

349.   "Education is the most powerful weapon which you can use to change the world" – Nelson Mandela

Date: _____

350.   "The only thing necessary for the triumph of evil is for good men to do nothing" – Edmund Burke

Date: _____

351.   "Life is 10% what happens to you and 90% how you react to it" – Charles R. Swindoll

Date: _____

352.   "Just as a candle cannot burn without fire, men cannot live without a spiritual life" - Buddha

Date: _____

RELATIONSHIP WITH OTHERS

353.   What are your thoughts on having a soul mate?

Date: _____

_____
_____
_____
_____
_____
_____
_____
_____
_____
_____

354.   What is the best gift you ever gave someone?

Date: _____

_____
_____
_____
_____
_____
_____
_____
_____
_____
_____
_____
_____

355.   Write down the three most important things you want in a relationship.

Date: _____

_____
_____
_____
_____
_____
_____
_____
_____
_____
_____
_____
_____

356.   What do you wish other people would do for you that they don't currently?

Date: _____

_____
_____
_____
_____
_____
_____
_____
_____
_____
_____
_____

357.   What would you like someone to say to you that they
       don't?

Date: _____

_____
_____
_____
_____
_____
_____
_____
_____
_____
_____
_____

358.   Describe your most compatible partner.

Date: _____

_____
_____
_____
_____
_____
_____
_____
_____
_____
_____
_____

359.   What makes a good friend?

Date: _____

_____
_____
_____
_____
_____
_____
_____
_____
_____
_____
_____
_____

360.   Describe the ultimate friendship.

Date: _____

_____
_____
_____
_____
_____
_____
_____
_____
_____
_____
_____
_____

361.   Write down how you are supportive to your friends

Date: _____

362.   Write about the different roles people play in your family.

Date: _____

363.   What person would describe you in the most positive way of all? What would the person say?

Date: _____

_____

_____

_____

_____

_____

_____

_____

_____

_____

_____

_____

_____

364.   What person would describe you in the most negative way? What would they say?

Date: _____

_____

_____

_____

_____

_____

_____

_____

_____

_____

_____

_____

365.   What is the best possible thing you could do for another person?

Date: _____

366.   Why do you think people act harmful?

Date: _____

367.   Make a list of how you can connect better and deeper with other people and revive your relationships

Date: _____

_____
_____
_____
_____
_____
_____
_____
_____
_____
_____
_____
_____

368.   Why do you think some conflicts are unsolvable?

Date: _____

_____
_____
_____
_____
_____
_____
_____
_____
_____
_____
_____
_____

YOU AND SOCIETY

369.   What do you think your society could learn from other
countries?

Date: _____

_____

_____

_____

_____

_____

_____

_____

_____

_____

_____

370.   What is the best thing your country does for its
inhabitants?

Date: _____

_____

_____

_____

_____

_____

_____

_____

_____

_____

_____

371.   What in society is shocking or offending to you?

Date: _____

_____

_____

_____

_____

_____

_____

_____

_____

_____

_____

372.   What five things would you change first of all if you were in charge?

Date: _____

_____

_____

_____

_____

_____

_____

_____

_____

_____

_____

373.   How would you describe your society in 10 sentences?

Date: _____

374.   What roles and work do you find most important in a society?

Date: _____

375. What would society be like tomorrow if there were no more TV or computers in all homes?

Date: _____

376. What would society actually be like in the future if there were no more drugs or alcohol to be found?

Date: _____

377.   Of all the people you know of, who do you think is worthy of leading your country and why?

Date: _____

_____
_____
_____
_____
_____
_____
_____
_____
_____
_____
_____
_____

378.   Write about events in history that have made a great impact on you.

Date: _____

_____
_____
_____
_____
_____
_____
_____
_____
_____
_____

379.   What life mysteries would you most like the answers to?
What do you think are the answers?

Date: _____

380.   If you could get rid of anything on the planet what would
it be?

Date: _____

381.   What do you wish more people knew about, and how would that change society?

Date: _____

382.   Write down pros and cons about the internet.

Date: _____

383.   What would you like to add to the school curriculum that kids are not currently taught?

Date: _____

_____

_____

_____

_____

_____

_____

_____

_____

_____

_____

_____

384.   If you could change the school system what would it look like?

Date: _____

_____

_____

_____

_____

_____

_____

_____

_____

_____

_____

_____

Finish the sentence:

385.   If I was in charge of this country I would first of all...

Date: _____

386.   The greatest downfalls of modern society...

Date: _____

TRAVELLING

387. What cultures are you drawn toward?

Date: _____

_____
_____
_____
_____
_____
_____
_____
_____
_____
_____
_____

388. What aspects of other cultures do you wish was also dominant in your culture?

Date: _____

_____
_____
_____
_____
_____
_____
_____
_____
_____
_____
_____

389.   What cultures would you like to experience that you have not yet seen?

Date: _____

_____

_____

_____

_____

_____

_____

_____

_____

_____

_____

390.   What would the ultimate travel experience be for you?

Date: _____

_____

_____

_____

_____

_____

_____

_____

_____

_____

_____

_____

391.   What languages would you like to speak and what is your current level in that language?

Date: _____

392.   Write about your best hotel experience.

Date: _____

393.   Write about the best travelling experience you ever had.

Date: _____

_____
_____
_____
_____
_____
_____
_____
_____
_____
_____

394.   Write down some traveling experiences you have had that you would like to have more of.

Date: _____

_____
_____
_____
_____
_____
_____
_____
_____
_____

395.   Write your thoughts on travelling of the grid with no electricity and no internet.

Date: _____

396.   If you could travel in time, when and where would you like to go and why?

Date: _____

397.   What kind of travelling do you not enjoy so much?

Date: _____

_____
_____
_____
_____
_____
_____
_____
_____
_____
_____

398.   What 5 countries do you most want to visit and what would you like to experience there?

Date: _____

_____
_____
_____
_____
_____
_____
_____
_____
_____
_____

MONEY AND FINANCES

399.   What are your thoughts about wealthy people?

Date: _____

_____

_____

_____

_____

_____

_____

_____

_____

_____

_____

_____

400.   What are your thoughts about money and wealth?

Date: _____

_____

_____

_____

_____

_____

_____

_____

_____

_____

_____

_____

401.   Who do you admire moneywise and why?

Date: _____

402.   Are there any wealthy persons you despise and why so?

Date: _____

403.   What did you hear and learn about money and wealth in
        your childhood?

Date: _____

_____
_____
_____
_____
_____
_____
_____
_____
_____
_____
_____
_____

404.   What conclusions did you make about money as a child?

Date: _____

_____
_____
_____
_____
_____
_____
_____
_____
_____
_____
_____
_____

405.   When was the first time you remember having any
money? What did you think about it?

Date: _____

_____
_____
_____
_____
_____
_____
_____
_____
_____
_____
_____
_____

406.   What are your financial goals?

Date: _____

_____
_____
_____
_____
_____
_____
_____
_____
_____
_____
_____
_____

407.   Why is it possible to reach wealth starting from scratch?

Date: _____

408.   How would it make you feel to reach your financial goals?

Date: _____

409.   What would it take for you to reach your financial goals?

Date: _____

410.   What's the reason you have not yet reached your goals?

Date: _____

411.   What do you need to be able to reach you financial goals?

Date: _____

412.   What would you like to earn money doing?

Date: _____

413.   What does money mean to you?

Date: _____

_____
_____
_____
_____
_____
_____
_____
_____
_____
_____
_____

414.   How do you feel about the subject of money?

Date: _____

_____
_____
_____
_____
_____
_____
_____
_____
_____
_____
_____

415.   Do you know anybody who is wealthy? What do you think
about them and their way with money?

Date: _____

_____
_____
_____
_____
_____
_____
_____
_____
_____
_____
_____

416.   What luxuries would you like to be able to afford?

Date: _____

_____
_____
_____
_____
_____
_____
_____
_____
_____
_____
_____

417.   Write a very long list of what would make you feel richer today.

Date: _____

418.   What are you afraid of doing relating to money?

Date: _____

419.   How can you improve your financial situation already today?

Date: _____

_____
_____
_____
_____
_____
_____
_____
_____
_____
_____

420.   What philanthropic causes or charities would you like to support financially?

Date: _____

_____
_____
_____
_____
_____
_____
_____
_____
_____
_____

421.   How could you spend less money?

Date: _____

_____
_____
_____
_____
_____
_____
_____
_____
_____
_____
_____

422.   What are the 5 next things you need to do to improve your financial situation?

Date: _____

_____
_____
_____
_____
_____
_____
_____
_____
_____
_____
_____

Write your thoughts on the following statements:

423.   "Money doesn't appear out of nowhere"

Date: _____

_____

_____

_____

_____

_____

_____

_____

_____

_____

_____

424.   "I have to work hard to make a lot of money"

Date: _____

_____

_____

_____

_____

_____

_____

_____

_____

_____

_____

425.   "No matter how much money I make, I never have enough"

Date: _____

426.   "I don't know enough about money to invest any"

Date: _____

CREATIVITY

427.   Write about a thing you created from scratch.

Date: _____

_____
_____
_____
_____
_____
_____
_____
_____
_____
_____
_____

428.   How do you like to express yourself creatively?

Date: _____

_____
_____
_____
_____
_____
_____
_____
_____
_____
_____

429.   In what way would you like to be more creative?

Date: _____

430.   How can you work on being more creative?

Date: _____

431.   Why should anyone be creative?

Date: _____

432.   Write down everything you can remember having created.

Date: _____

433.   Write down what you are most proud of having created and why.

Date: _____

_____
_____
_____
_____
_____
_____
_____
_____
_____
_____
_____

434.   Who is the most creative person you know and what makes him or her creative?

Date: _____

_____
_____
_____
_____
_____
_____
_____
_____
_____
_____
_____

435.   Which art forms are you attracted to and what do you like about them?

Date: _____

436.   What is the greatest thing you could possibly create?

Date: _____

437.   Write down 5 things that have inspired you to be creative.

Date: _____

438.   Which artistic skills would you like to improve on?

Date: _____

FINDING YOUR PASSION

439.　　If you could teach any topic to a school class what would it be?

Date: _____

_____
_____
_____
_____
_____
_____
_____
_____
_____
_____

440.　　What courses - real or imaginary - would you love to take?

Date: _____

_____
_____
_____
_____
_____
_____
_____
_____
_____
_____
_____

441.   What wouldn't you mind doing for free just because you
enjoy it?

Date: _____

442.   What activities makes you feel alive?

Date: _____

443.   What would you do if you only had 8 more years to live?

Date: _____

_____
_____
_____
_____
_____
_____
_____
_____
_____
_____

444.   What would you like to have more of in your work right now?

Date: _____

_____
_____
_____
_____
_____
_____
_____
_____
_____
_____

445.   What would you like to have less of in your work right now?

Date: _____

_____
_____
_____
_____
_____
_____
_____
_____
_____
_____
_____

446.   What do you get the most compliments for?

Date: _____

_____
_____
_____
_____
_____
_____
_____
_____
_____
_____
_____

447.   What do you consider your 3 biggest talents?

Date: _____

448.   What 3 areas do you know most about?

Date: _____

449.   What 3 areas are you most interested in?

Date: _____

450.   What kind of problems do you most like to solve?

Date: _____

451.   What areas do you most like to help people with?

Date: _____

_____

_____

_____

_____

_____

_____

_____

_____

_____

_____

452.   What king of blog would you like to have if any?

Date: _____

_____

_____

_____

_____

_____

_____

_____

_____

_____

_____

453.   What did you love to do as a child (age 3-12)?

Date: _____

_____
_____
_____
_____
_____
_____
_____
_____
_____
_____

454.   If you could choose freely, in which company or organization would you most like work?

Date: _____

_____
_____
_____
_____
_____
_____
_____
_____
_____
_____
_____
_____

455.   If you didn't have to work for money what would you most
like to volunteer for?

Date: _____

456.   What do you often find yourself promoting to others?

Date: _____

Finish the sentence:

457.   As a teenager, I loved to...

Date: _____

_____
_____
_____
_____
_____
_____
_____
_____
_____
_____
_____

458.   As a child, I dreamed of becoming...

Date: _____

_____
_____
_____
_____
_____
_____
_____
_____
_____
_____

459.   As a teenager, I dreamed of becoming...

Date: _____

460.   In my early 20s, I dreamed of becoming...

Date: _____

MAKING A LIFE VISION

461.   How would you most like to live?

Date: _____

_____
_____
_____
_____
_____
_____
_____
_____
_____
_____
_____

462.   Where would you most like to live?

Date: _____

_____
_____
_____
_____
_____
_____
_____
_____
_____
_____
_____
_____

463.   Describe how a nearly perfect average day for you would be like.

Date: _____

_____
_____
_____
_____
_____
_____
_____
_____
_____
_____
_____

464.   What do you believe your highest potential is?

Date: _____

_____
_____
_____
_____
_____
_____
_____
_____
_____
_____
_____

465.   Write down your own ultimate most desired response to the question "what do you do for a living?"

Date: _____

_____

466.   Write your obituary.

Date: _____

467.   What does your life look like one year from now?

Date: _____

_____
_____
_____
_____
_____
_____
_____
_____
_____
_____

468.   What does your life look like 3 years from now?

Date: _____

_____
_____
_____
_____
_____
_____
_____
_____
_____
_____
_____

469.   Write about the things you feel you must soon do otherwise it will be too late.

Date: _____

_____
_____
_____
_____
_____
_____
_____
_____
_____
_____

470.   What do you have to do to not have any regrets later in life?

Date: _____

_____
_____
_____
_____
_____
_____
_____
_____
_____
_____

471.   What do you want to have written on you tomb stone?

Date: _____

_____
_____
_____
_____
_____
_____
_____
_____
_____
_____

472.   What is your purpose in life?

Date: _____

_____
_____
_____
_____
_____
_____
_____
_____
_____
_____

473.   What would you like to give to the world?

Date: _____

474.   Where would you be in one year from now, if you DON'T take any action?

Date: _____

475.   What would you like to experience?

Date: _____

_____
_____
_____
_____
_____
_____
_____
_____
_____
_____

476.   What kind of activity out of your comfort zone would you like to engage in?

Date: _____

_____
_____
_____
_____
_____
_____
_____
_____
_____
_____

477.   Where would you be in 5 years if you didn't take any
action towards your dreams?

Date: _____

_____
_____
_____
_____
_____
_____
_____
_____
_____
_____
_____

478.   What's the worst that could happen if you went for your
dream?

Date: _____

_____
_____
_____
_____
_____
_____
_____
_____
_____
_____

479.   What's the best that could happen if you went for your dream?

Date: _____

_____
_____
_____
_____
_____
_____
_____
_____
_____
_____

480.   What are your current excuses for not following your dream?

Date: _____

_____
_____
_____
_____
_____
_____
_____
_____
_____

481.   Whom or what do you blame for your current situation?

Date: _____

482.   What would the people you admire advice you to do next?

Date: _____

483.   Describe how you can know that you are on the right path of life.

Date: _____

_____
_____
_____
_____
_____
_____
_____
_____
_____
_____
_____

484.   If you had one year left to live, what would you change immediately?

Date: _____

_____
_____
_____
_____
_____
_____
_____
_____
_____
_____
_____

IMPROVING YOUR HEALTH

485.   If your body had a voice what would it tell you?

Date: _____

486.   Describe would you would like your daily health routine to be.

Date: _____

487.   Write about the time in your life you felt most healthy.

Date: _____

488.   What is good health to you?

Date: _____

489.   Who do you consider very healthy and why?

Date: _____

490.   How could you realistically become healthier?

Date: _____

491.   How would you teach health to a child? What would you
say and advice?

Date: _____

492.   Write down the best well-balanced diet for you.

Date: _____

START
DREAMING
BIG

493.   List some costly things you would like to buy over the next 12 months.

Date: _____

_____

_____

_____

_____

_____

_____

_____

_____

_____

_____

_____

494.   Write down how you would spend $100.000 if you only had one day to do it in.

Date: _____

_____

_____

_____

_____

_____

_____

_____

_____

_____

_____

495.   Write down the perfect life-scenario for you three years
        from now.

Date: _____

_____

_____

_____

_____

_____

_____

_____

_____

_____

_____

_____

496.   What would you like to wear daily if everything was
        possible?

Date: _____

_____

_____

_____

_____

_____

_____

_____

_____

_____

_____

_____

497.   What' is absolutely unrealistic and why?

Date: _____

498.   How would you like to decorate your home if you didn't have to think about anybody else's opinion?

Date: _____

499.   What wildly luxurious things could you imagine enjoying?

Date: _____

_____
_____
_____
_____
_____
_____
_____
_____
_____
_____

500.   If you won 2 million dollars, what dreams would you most certainly make real?

Date: _____

_____
_____
_____
_____
_____
_____
_____
_____
_____
_____